GLACIER
NATIONAL PARK

JENNY MARKERT
THE CHILD'S WORLD

Designed and Photographed by:
MICHAEL GEORGE

Distributed to schools and libraries in the United States by
ENCYCLOPAEDIA BRITANNICA EDUCATIONAL CORP.
310 South Michigan Avenue
Chicago, Illinois 60604

Library of Congress Cataloging-in-Publication Data
Markert, Jenny.
Glacier National Park / by Jenny Markert.
p. cm.
Summary: Describes a backpack trip through Glacier
National Park and introduces the area's natural history,
biology, and geology.
ISBN 0-89565-858-5
1. Glacier National Park (Mont.)--Juvenile literature.
2. Natural history--Montana--Glacier National Park--
Juvenile literature.
[1. Glacier National Park (Mont.)   2. National parks and
reserves.]   I. Title.
F737.G5M37   1993   92-4262
917.86'52--dc20   CIP
                                                              AC

Driving from Minnesota to Montana, few things rise above the flat, grassy plains. The horizon is sometimes broken by a billboard or a church steeple, but little else. Two-thirds the way across Montana, I thought I saw mountains on the distant horizon. Or were they storm clouds hovering above the ground? I argued with myself for the next half hour. Fifty miles from Glacier National Park, I finally decided that lofty mountains did indeed lie ahead.

For the next hour, the mountains gradually closed in around us. We soon passed the entrance to Glacier National Park. Steep peaks surrounded the park like stone walls guarding a castle. The mountains were not dry and brittle like others I had seen. They grabbed my attention as only real mountains could. The slopes were painted with dark gray rocks and deep green pines. The peaks were rough and jagged, as if sculpted by an impatient artist.

We turned off the pavement onto a bumpy dirt road. We were headed toward Bowman Lake Campground. The lake was about 35 miles away, but it was one of the only campgrounds that still had vacant sites. The road was

Later that morning, we packed up the car and left the rugged wilderness of Glacier National Park. As we headed east, I watched the mountains gradually shrink in the rearview mirror. I felt disappointed but also relieved. The plains were still flat and featureless, but they promised another two months of summer before the winds of winter would begin to blow.

《————————》

THE CHILD'S WORLD
NATUREBOOKS

Wildlife Library

Alligators	Musk-oxen
Arctic Foxes	Octopuses
Bald Eagles	Owls
Beavers	Penguins
Birds	Polar Bears
Black Widows	Primates
Camels	Rattlesnakes
Cheetahs	Reptiles
Coyotes	Rhinoceroses
Dogs	Seals and Sea Lions
Dolphins	Sharks
Elephants	Snakes
Fish	Spiders
Giraffes	Tigers
Insects	Walruses
Kangaroos	Whales
Lions	Wildcats
Mammals	Wolves
Monarchs	Zebras

Space Library

Earth	The Moon
Mars	The Sun

Adventure Library

Glacier National Park	Yosemite
The Grand Canyon	Yellowstone National Park

covered with dirt and exhausted from the day-long hike. We camped right on shore, nestled among rugged mountains and tall pine trees. The lake's glassy surface was disturbed only by the wake of a loon.

I dozed to sleep as the sky grew dark. Hours later, I woke to a brilliant, star-filled sky. The stars were brighter than I had ever seen. They seemed so close. The distinct band of the Milky Way arched across the sky. I stayed awake for an hour, making wishes on all the falling stars.

I expected to wake up the next morning to blue skies, but every camper knows that few things turn out as planned. Instead of the sun, the pitter patter of raindrops greeted us at dawn. A steady rain was falling from a thick cover of clouds.

We had food for only one night, so we were forced to hike back in the rain. We trudged up the muddy trail in our squishy boots and wet clothes. It was chilly, but the rain wasn't so bad. In fact, it was kind of fun. Since we were already wet, we could stomp through the mud puddles and not even care! I heard the rain's symphony between the squish-squash of my boots. It gently tapped on the bushes and trees. The leaves seemed to grow greener before my eyes.

rough and winding, so our progress was slow. Fortunately, there was no lack of scenery. Flowers glistened by the roadside and deer bounded through the trees. In the distance, towering mountains still showed signs of the last winter's snow.

By the time we reached Bowman Lake, our necks were stiff and the car was covered with dust. We stood up, stretched, and headed to the lake. The surface was quiet and still. Smooth, flat rocks covered the shore. We stood at the water's edge, skipping rocks and watching the ripples spread across the surface. Our wet shoes brought plea-sure that only a true rock skipper could appreciate.

The sun soon slipped below a distant ridge. The western hillsides caught the sunset's subtle hues—pastel pinks, purples, and blues. As night crept in, every color grew brighter and more distinct. Then, quite suddenly, it was dark.

The next morning we left the picnic tables of Bowman Lake in search of a less civilized campground. Our destination was Quartz Lake, a remote hideaway that can be reached only by foot. The trail entered a dim forest covered by a canopy of pines. The path was soft and scented. It was carpeted by a thick layer of pine needles.

We reached the edge of Quartz Lake late in the afternoon. We were

The rain was still falling when we reached the car. Our clothes were soaked and our skin was wrinkled. Trying to dry off and change clothes in the car made it difficult to smile. Sleeping all night in a wet tent made it impossible.

We spent the next morning at the laundromat, drying our clothes and mending our spirits. When we ran out of quarters, we hopped in the car and rolled down the windows. The rain had stopped and the sun was shining. To celebrate, we drove up Glacier Park's only thoroughfare, Going-to-the-Sun Road. Luckily, I was a passenger and could devote my full attention to the passing scenery.

We started near Lake McDonald, a scenic lake bordered by a steep-sided valley. Lush vegetation clung to the rocky walls. Countless waterfalls plummeted to the lake below. As the lake disappeared behind us, the mountains around us seemed to grow. The higher we climbed, the more spectacular they became.

I could easily pick out where glaciers sat, ages and ages ago. Though there are still some glaciers in the park, they are not nearly so awesome as they once were. About 3 million years ago, a series of great ice ages advanced on Glacier Park. During each ice age, summers were short and winters were long. Snow and ice piled up year after year.

As the ice grew thicker, it began to slide downhill, forming massive rivers of ice. The glaciers slowly carved the steep-sided valleys that are visible today.

Though it sometimes snows in July or August, the climate in Glacier Park is not nearly as cold as it once was. Many animals inhabit the park year round, including a variety of large plant-eaters. Moose browse near grassy lake shores and marshes. Elk and deer wander the hillsides and forests. Big-horn sheep live near the mountain tops in summer, but descend to warmer valleys in the winter. Mountain goats stay on the highest, windiest peaks year round. They are expert rock climbers, and can scamper up or down the steepest cliffs. The terrain they live on is so severe that predators rarely pursue them.

Animals that live at lower elevations must be wary of a variety of predators. Mountain lions, bobcats, and lynx stalk the woods and riverbeds for prey. Many bears also live in Glacier Park. Black bears are the most common species, though grizzlies also roam the hills. Both types of bear feed on roots and berries, but prefer a meal of fresh meat. When it comes to humans, most bears would rather retreat than attack. Fortunately, we never had to test that theory. As is true for most visitors, we didn't see any bears during our hikes through Glacier Park.

The most troublesome creatures we encountered in Glacier Park were some leery ground squirrels. A whole network of squirrel holes dotted the trail to Iceberg Lake. In front of us, the cautious rodents darted into the safety of their homes. Then they would peek out and whistle to warn their friends that we were coming.

The small birds that hopped from tree to tree were much more cordial than the squirrels. They sang their cheery songs as if to welcome us. Bigger birds soared on the air currents high above our heads. Wildflowers covered the adjacent hillsides. Every flower had its own color and a butter-fly that matched!

At the top of the trail, jagged peaks proudly cradled Iceberg Lake. Even in the middle of July, the lake lived up to its name. It was filled with giant slabs of ice. That high in the mountains, it takes most of the summer to melt the ice that forms each winter. Between the chunks of ice, we could see chalky, blue-green water. The color was caused by suspended *glacial silt*—fine powder that ancient glaciers scraped from the surrounding mountains.

We spent one more night in Glacier Park. The next morning, the air was was stiff and cold. The mountain peaks were covered with a frosting of snow. Though it was July, winter was already warning of its approach.